Red Flag Translator

Sarah Melland

Disclaimer:

The content of this book is for entertainment purposes only. The author and publisher are not responsible for any actions or consequences arising from the use or application of the information provided in this book. All views expressed are personal and should not be construed as professional advice.

Table of Contents

"He wasn't a mistake — he was the mirror that made you dangerous."

Introduction

Welcome to the Red Flag Translator — your ultimate guide to decoding the nonsense in modern dating. You've probably already encountered a few red flags that made you squint at your phone and wonder, *"Wait... am I being played?"* Well, darling, you probably are.

This book exists to help you spot those red flags before they turn into full-on deal-breakers. Because let's face it — dating today can feel like walking through a field of red flags with a blindfold on. But it doesn't have to be that way.

Here's the deal: Men (and let's be real, some women) have mastered the art of saying just enough to keep you interested, but not enough to make any real commitment. They toss out a lot of talk, some charm, maybe a sweet emoji or two, and suddenly, you're wondering if you're the crazy one for questioning their intentions. But no, honey. You're not crazy. You're just paying attention. And in this book, we're going to teach you how to pay even better attention.

How to Use This Book

This book is for you if you've ever been confused by a text that felt like it came from a cryptic puzzle master. It's for the woman who's sick of endlessly analyzing every single word someone says. It's for the ones who are tired of ignoring their gut feeling in the name of *giving him a chance*. You deserve better than that.

Each chapter is packed with Red Flags — real examples of behaviors, phrases, and mind games that we've all seen (or unfortunately experienced) in the wild world of dating. I'm breaking it all down for you: what he says, what he *really* means, and how to handle it without second-guessing yourself. These red flags? They're NOT your problem anymore. This book will help you put them in the rearview mirror.

The beauty of this book is simple: You don't need to spend hours dissecting texts and awkward conversations. I've done the dirty work for you. You'll get straight-to-the-point translations and *UnExpert Tips* to handle these situations like the confident, no-nonsense woman you are.

So, buckle up. We're about to translate that mess into clarity, and trust me, after reading this, you'll never miss another red flag again. You'll spot them from a mile away and swipe left — with confidence — every single time.

And ladies, while I still have your attention, this isn't doomsday. After every chapter, I have how to be iconic with these men. So don't give up on dating, but definitely have fun, not every man is out to get you or teach you a life-altering lesson.

Let's dive in.

Part One: Understanding Red Flags

What Are Red Flags?

In the world of dating, red flags are signs — and I mean *bright*, blaring signs — that something isn't right. They're the behaviors, comments, or patterns that make you pause, squint, and wonder if your date has a secret alter ego.

Red flags can be big, obvious things like *he says he's "not ready for a relationship" but acts like he's auditioning for the role of your future husband*. They can also be small, sneaky things like *him canceling plans last-minute and then acting like it's no big deal*. But no matter the size, a red flag is a signal that something's off. And here's the kicker: **Ignoring it doesn't make it go away.**

Just like you wouldn't ignore a flashing red light while driving (unless you've *really* got a death wish), ignoring red flags in relationships can lead you straight into a mess of emotional traffic. Red flags aren't meant to be *debated* or *explained away* by your inner optimism — they're meant to be **acknowledged** and **acted upon**. Trust me, your intuition has been doing its job, and it's time to start listening to it.

The Psychology Behind Red Flags

Now, let's talk about why we miss red flags — even when they're waving right in front of us. Here's the deal: **Humans are wired to avoid discomfort**, and the idea of confronting an issue or walking away from someone we're attracted to can be way harder than it seems. When we see a red flag, we don't always want to believe it. It's easier to

3

excuse the behavior, chalk it up to a bad day, or think *"He's just going through a rough time."*

But, let's be clear: This isn't about *excusing* bad behavior. This is about **denying** it.

The psychology behind ignoring red flags is deeply rooted in **cognitive dissonance**, which is basically the discomfort we feel when we have two conflicting thoughts. For example: You might be *really into him*, but deep down, you know he's **not treating you right**. So, instead of facing the discomfort, we try to resolve that tension by justifying his behavior or ignoring the warning signs.

Here's the thing, though: The longer you deny these red flags, the more they compound. One small red flag becomes a bigger, more difficult situation down the road. That's why the key to handling them is noticing them early — and acting on them *before* they become patterns.

Why This Book Exists

Let's face it, dating today is like navigating a field of landmines in a blindfold. The modern dating world is full of mixed signals, emotional games, and manipulation tactics that can leave you second-guessing yourself at every turn. You're not alone if you've felt confused or frustrated by the dating process. This book exists to put an end to that.

I'm here to help you decode the **games**, the **phrases**, and the **red flags** that you've been brushing off. With this book, you'll finally have a **toolkit** to understand what the heck is actually happening in your dating life, and how to spot the signs *before* they pull you into a whirlwind of emotional chaos.

By the time you finish, you won't just be able to spot a red flag — you'll see it coming from a mile away. You'll know exactly what it means, how to handle it, and most importantly, how to protect your time, energy, and heart.

This book is for the women who are **done** second-guessing their intuition. It's for the ones who are tired of tolerating behavior that makes them feel confused, drained, or emotionally unavailable. This is for you — the bold, confident woman who's done putting up with nonsense and ready to level up in her dating life.

Let's face it: We all deserve more than breadcrumbs and mixed signals. It's time to make the right choices, **right now**, before you waste any more time on the wrong people.

Part 2: The Red Flags

Chapter 1: Profile Text Red Flags

Where the nonsense begins — before he even messages you.

Let's be honest — most dating app profiles are less "carefully crafted personal intros" and more "emotionally unhinged marketing copy." The bio is the first look into who he *thinks* he is, who he *wants* you to believe he is, or what kind of chaos he's quietly warning you about.

And that's why this chapter matters: **His profile is his pitch.**

And just like with any pitch, if he's overselling, overcompensating, or already sounding bitter — believe him.

This is where you'll find the **passive aggression wrapped in sarcasm**, the **fake vulnerability hidden behind one-liners**, and the ever-classic "I'm 6'2 because apparently that matters" energy. Sometimes they're trying to look deep, funny, or mysterious. Other times, they're **clearly just tired of women altogether but still want someone to make their bed**.

The red flags in a profile text are often the most **ignored** because they're packaged as jokes or "just honesty." But here's your golden rule:

> *If it feels off at the intro stage — it's not going to get better from here.*

Now let's decode the bios that should make you put down your phone, take a breath, and swipe left with confidence.

📢 What He Says:

"No drama."

🐱 What He Actually Means:

"I've never taken accountability in my life, and the second you have feelings, I'll call you crazy."

🔻 UnExpert Tip:
When a man says "no drama," he's usually the one bringing it.
It's not a boundary — it's a preemptive gaslight.

📢 What He Says:

"Looking for my partner in crime."

🐱 What He Actually Means:

"I've put zero thought into this and just reused a line from every man who's ever existed."

🔻 UnExpert Tip:
If he's using clichés, expect copy-paste behavior in the relationship too.

📢 What He Says:

"Just ask."

🐱 What He Actually Means:

"I'm too lazy to write a single sentence, but I expect you to be intrigued anyway."

🔻 UnExpert Tip:
This is not mystery. This is effort-avoidant energy disguised as cool guy minimalism.

📢 What He Says:

"Not looking for anything serious."

🐻 What He Actually Means:

"I will absolutely treat you like a girlfriend until you ask me what we are."

🔻 UnExpert Tip:
He's telling you upfront. Believe him. And run.

📢 What He Says:

"I'm a nice guy."

🐻 What He Actually Means:

"I think I deserve your time just because I'm not actively committing crimes."

🔻 UnExpert Tip:
If he *has* to tell you he's nice, he's probably not.

📢 What He Says:

"Fluent in sarcasm."

🐻 What He Actually Means:

"I've never developed real emotional communication skills and will probably neg you to flirt."

🔻 UnExpert Tip:
Sarcasm isn't a personality. Neither is being emotionally stunted.

🔊 What He Says:

"I'm a nice guy."

🦫 What He Actually Means:

"I think I deserve your time just because I'm not actively committing crimes."

🔻 UnExpert Tip:
If he *has* to tell you he's nice, he's probably not.

🔊 What He Says:

"6', because apparently that matters."

🦫 What He Actually Means:

"I'm salty about dating apps and I have a chip on my shoulder... but it's over 6 feet tall."

🔻 UnExpert Tip:
Height doesn't make up for bitterness. Or basic respect.

🔊 What He Says:

"Don't waste my time."

🦫 What He Actually Means:

"I'm already bitter and projecting it onto strangers on the internet."

🔻 UnExpert Tip:
If he's leading with resentment, you'll be defending yourself by the second date.

📣 What He Says:

"I'm brutally honest."

🐸 What He Actually Means:

"I'm rude, emotionally reckless, and think tact is for weak men."

🔻 UnExpert Tip:
Brutal honesty is usually just brutality in a nicer font.

📣 What He Says:

"If you can't handle me at my worst..."

🐸 What He Actually Means:

"I have no plans to grow as a person. Please accept my emotional chaos as-is."

🔻 UnExpert Tip:
He's not deep — he's just exhausting.

📣 What He Says:

"Work hard, play harder."

🐸 What He Actually Means:

"I drink like I'm still in college and have zero time for you Monday–Friday."

🔻 UnExpert Tip:
If his life sounds like a Red Bull ad, you'll be the one burned out.

📢 What He Says:

"Sapiosexual."

🦝 What He Actually Means:

"I Googled the word 'sapiosexual' once and now I think it makes me interesting."

🔻 UnExpert Tip:
If he can't spell it or explain it, he's not it.

📢 What He Says:

"I'm not here to play games."

🦝 What He Actually Means:

"I will ghost you, breadcrumb you, and come back three weeks later like nothing happened."

🔻 UnExpert Tip:
This line is the opening move to a long, messy game.

📢 What He Says:

"Swipe right if you're not crazy."

🦝 What He Actually Means:

"I drove my last three exes into an emotional spiral and now I pretend it was their fault."

🔻 UnExpert Tip:
Any man who uses the word "crazy" as a personality filter *is* the red flag.

📢 What He Says:

"Let's vibe."

🐻 What He Actually Means:

"I have no plan, no depth, no accountability — but I do own LED lights."

🔻 UnExpert Tip:
Vibes are not a relationship strategy. They're a TikTok lighting setting.

📢 What He Says:

"My love language is touch."

🐻 What He Actually Means:

"I have one move and it's trying to put my hand on your thigh during appetizers."

🔻 UnExpert Tip:
If touch is his only love language, prepare to be touched... not loved.

📢 What He Says:

"I don't chase."

🐻 What He Actually Means:

"I expect you to do all the emotional labor while I contribute memes and eye contact."

🔻 UnExpert Tip:
Translation: lazy, entitled, and already checked out.

📣 What He Says:

"Wifey material only."

🐻 What He Actually Means:

"I want a woman who cooks, cleans, and heals my inner child... while I give the bare minimum."

🔻 UnExpert Tip:
If he's looking for a wife, but acting like a teenager, you're not the problem.

📣 What He Says:

"No 420? No chance."

🐻 What He Actually Means:

"My entire personality revolves around weed and I think that's a flex."

🔻 UnExpert Tip:
If he's dating his vape pen, there's no room left for you.

📣 What He Says:

"Here for a good time, not a long time."

🐻 What He Actually Means:

"I'm going to ruin your life for 2-3 business days and vanish."

🔻 UnExpert Tip:
You'll see his reflection in a tequila shot, not in your future.

📢 What He Says:

"I'm not like other guys."

🐻 What He Actually Means:

"I'm exactly like the last guy who said this to you — but somehow worse at texting."

🔻 UnExpert Tip:
If he has to tell you he's different, he isn't.

📢 What He Says:

"I've been hurt before."

🐻 What He Actually Means:

"I haven't healed, and now you get to clean up the emotional mess."

🔻 UnExpert Tip:
You're not his rehab center. You're a woman. Walk away.

📢 What He Says:

"Looking for a queen to build an empire with."

🐻 What He Actually Means:

"I run a barely legal drop-shipping business and need a ride to FedEx."

🔻 UnExpert Tip:
He's not building an empire — he's building debt and daddy issues.

🔊 What He Says:

"If you ghost me, you'll regret it."

🗣 What He Actually Means:

*"I'm deeply unwell and might Venmo you $0.01 just to say 'f** you."*

🔻 UnExpert Tip:
You don't need closure. You need a restraining order.

🔊 What He Says:

"Not looking for pen pals."

🗣 What He Actually Means:

"If you don't meet me within 3 messages, I'll emotionally retaliate."

🔻 UnExpert Tip:
He doesn't want connection — he wants compliance.

🔊 What He Says:

"I'll treat you like a princess... if you earn it."

🗣 What He Actually Means:

"I'm emotionally manipulative with a sprinkle of toxic conditional love."

🔻 UnExpert Tip:
Love isn't a rewards program. Next.

📢 What He Says:

"I'm an alpha."

🧟 What He Actually Means:

"I got rejected once in 2014 and now I follow podcast bros for guidance."

🔻 UnExpert Tip:
If he says "alpha," he's probably allergic to therapy.

📢 What He Says:

"Don't be boring."

🧟 What He Actually Means:

"I expect you to entertain me because I have no personality of my own."

🔻 UnExpert Tip:
If you wanted a clown, just say that.

📢 What He Says:

"Prove to me you're different."

🧟 What He Actually Means:

"You're now competing with the ghosts of every woman I didn't heal from."

🔻 UnExpert Tip:
You're not here to prove anything — especially to a man with three

📢 What He Sends:

"Send a pic?"

🐻 What He Actually Means:

"I want instant gratification but won't remember your birthday."

🔻 UnExpert Tip:
If the first thing he wants is a photo — the last thing he'll give is effort.

How to Date These Men and Still Win

AKA: How to Swipe Like a Savage and Still Get the Crown

Let's be honest — most profiles read like a walking red flag parade. But if you're going to give one of these men a chance (because hey, we've all swiped out of boredom), here's how to do it without losing your dignity — or your time.

1. Use His Bio as a Blueprint — Not a Dealbreaker

He says "No drama"? Cool. Then you set the tone from day one: calm confidence, no chase. The second he flips and brings *actual* drama, you disappear like he never happened.

👑 *The savage sets the vibe, not the man.*

2. Make Him Work to Keep Your Attention

He gave you four words and a fishing photo? Reply with a compliment on the fish… then say nothing else. If he wants more, he'll come correct or swim upstream.

💬 *Less effort from him = less access to you.*

3. Reply With a Mirror, Not a Monologue

When he says something basic or bitter ("Don't waste my time"), hit him with:

"You usually lead with that line?" *Or* "Wow, who hurt you?"
Watch him either soften or expose the full clown. Either way, *you win.*

4. Out-Match His Mystery

If he wrote nothing? Don't even *try* to carry the convo. Match his nothing with nothing. If he messages you later, act like you've never seen his profile.

👀 *Icon behavior: unbothered, unmatched, unforgettable.*

5. Reward Clarity, Ignore Confusion

Any man who's upfront, intentional, and actually writes a real bio — *praise that man.* Start the conversation. Engage. Make it known you're here for connection, not games.

💎 *Being savage doesn't mean being cold. It means being selective.*

Final Word for the Chapter 1 Girlies:

You're not here to fix a man with a bad bio. You're here to **filter**.
You are not "just another match." You are the standard.

Swipe with discernment. Respond with power.
And remember: *if you feel even a flicker of "ew," trust it and move on.*

Chapter 2: Messaging Red Flags

Welcome to the world of *texting*, *DMs*, and *voice memos* — the land of *"Hey"*, *"You up?"*, and *"Why aren't you answering me?"*. If you've been navigating dating apps, social media, or just the modern world of digital romance, you know that messaging can make or break a relationship before it even starts.

It's the first place where you can spot those sneaky little red flags. We've all been there — texting with someone who seems *great* at first, only to realize that their messages are more confusing than a jumbled puzzle.

Does he **actually** like you, or is he just bored? Why is he texting you at 2 a.m. with a "You up?" instead of *"How was your day?"* And what does it mean when the messages get weirdly vague or disappear for days on end? Are you *too clingy* for wondering why he hasn't responded, or is he gaslighting you into thinking it's your fault?

This chapter is all about those early signs that something is **off** in the way someone communicates. Whether it's the **lazy texter** who can't hold a conversation, the **breadcrumbing pro** who sends just enough to keep you hanging on, or the **ghosting king** who disappears without explanation, messaging can be a minefield. But the good news is, once you know the red flags to look out for, you'll never have to second-guess your text convos again.

Let's break down the most common **Messaging Red Flags**, what they really mean, and how you can protect yourself from falling into the traps they set. Trust me, once you spot these signals, you'll be dodging them like a pro — no more getting tangled in confusing texts or mind games.

📢 What He Says:

"I'm not a big fan of small talk…"

🐻 What He Actually Means:

"I'm emotionally lazy, and I'm not interested in actually getting to know you beyond surface-level questions that require no effort."

🔻 UnExpert Tip:

If someone can't handle small talk, they can't handle real talk. It's code for *I'm not actually invested in this date.*

📢 What He Sends:

The Three Dots... *(that never lead to a reply)*

🐻 What He Actually Means:

"I'm emotionally stalling because I don't know what I want, and this is a power move to keep you waiting."

🔻 UnExpert Tip:

If the dots don't lead to anything, it's because he's waiting for your emotional response to *fuel* his ego. I feel like this is an intentional control move. Breadcrumbing mixed with emotional ghosting.

📢 What He Says:

"Let's skip the small talk."

🐱 What He Actually Means:

"I'm gonna trauma dump or ask what turns you on within five messages."

🔻 UnExpert Tip:
There's nothing deep about emotionally speed-running intimacy.

📢 What He Sends:

He hearts your message instead of replying.

🐱 What He Actually Means:

"I want to let you know I saw your text without actually engaging in a meaningful conversation."

🔻 UnExpert Tip:
Oh my God, is there anything more annoying? Especially when you ask a question. A "heart" is a lazy cop-out. It's not *communication* — it's *signal confusion.*

📢 What He Sends:

Voice memo at 2 a.m.

🐱 What He Actually Means:

"I don't want to call you, but I'll send a voice memo at an inconvenient time because I think it'll make you feel special."

🔻 UnExpert Tip:
If it's 2 a.m., and he's dropping a voice memo — the only thing *real*

How to Date These Men and Still Win

AKA: The Art of Texting Like a High-Value Savage

So, he sends "wyd" at 11:42 p.m. He hearts your message instead of replying. He says "Let's skip the small talk" and trauma dumps by message three. Cute. Let's teach him how to spell *regret*.

1. Respond When It's Convenient — Not When It's Emotional

Stop treating his every buzz like a bat signal.
If he sends lazy messages, you take your time — *hours or days*. Not to play games, but to show that your energy has *premium placement*.
⚱ *You're not his entertainment. You're the prize he forgot to earn.*

2. Give His Breadcrumbs to the Birds

He's giving one-word answers? Dry energy? "👀" with no follow-up?
Cool. Respond with a *screenshot* to your group chat, not a reply to him.
◳ *If he's not giving you dialogue, he doesn't deserve your character arc.*

3. Use Humor to Expose the Lazy

He hits you with "Hey" or "You up?"
Your response: "Wow. A full sentence. Is this a slow reveal or are we skipping straight to the part where I ignore you?"

Let him feel your vibe shift through the WiFi.
👊 *You don't ghost — you haunt.*

4. Mirror Energy, But Make It Icy Luxe

If he hearts your question instead of answering it?
Next time he asks something, reply with:

"💜"

That's it. Deadpan. No follow-up. Watch him spiral.

💬 *Emotional minimalism? We can match it. But ours comes with high heels and consequences.*

5. Don't Reward Inconsistency with Intimacy

If he disappears and reappears, act like you don't remember him. Literally:

"Sorry, new phone — who dis?"

If you want a more savage approach because that line may be overplayed, here are a few more:

"You again? I thought I unsubscribed."

👉 Cold. Corporate. Emotionally unavailable.

"Didn't recognize your number without the lies attached."

👉 Stabs with elegance.

"You're not blocked?"

👉 Meta-spiritual warfare.

"Took me a sec. I had to scroll past my standards to find you."

👉 A little petty. A lot powerful.

"Oh. You still have signal down there?"

👉 Deliciously degrading.

"Did you forget you're a lesson?"

👉 Straight from the red flag scriptures.

"Oh, it's you. My closure in human form."

👉 Punchline + period.

"I'd ask what you want, but I finally stopped caring."

👉 Calm. Cruel. Complete.

🔕 *Every time you re-engage a lazy texter, you're auditioning for his rotation. Withdraw the application.*

Final Word for the Chapter 2 Girlies:

If a man can't impress you in *text,* where he has full control of timing, words, and spellcheck — do you really think he's going to pull up in real life with flowers and emotional intelligence?

You are not a reply girl.
You are the *main event*.
Let him earn every single key you press.

Chapter 3: Behavioral Red Flags

He says one thing, but the vibes say otherwise.

This is where the red flags stop being cute little quotes on a profile and start **showing up in his actual behavior**. These are the patterns, inconsistencies, and "huh?" moments that don't always come with flashing lights — but they *should*. He's texting you every day... until he's not. He talks about wanting something real... but only after midnight. He compliments your confidence... until you actually use your voice.

Behavioral red flags are the most dangerous kind because they require *you* to notice the **gap between what he says and what he does**. And if you've ever been gaslit, lovebombed, or breadcrumbed into second-guessing yourself, you know that gap can feel like your fault. It's not.

This chapter is your decoder ring for the actions (or lack thereof) that tell you *exactly* where he stands — no matter what his mouth says. You'll learn how to clock inconsistency, detect emotional unavailability in disguise, and call BS on the guys who talk like boyfriends but move like strangers.

Because if his behavior has you confused, anxious, or questioning your worth — that's not "taking things slow." That's a red flag waving in broad daylight.
Let's break it down.

📢 What He Says:

"You intimidate me."

🐸 What He Actually Means:

"You have boundaries, goals, and confidence — and I have no idea how to handle that."

🔻 UnExpert Tip:
Don't shrink for a man who can't grow.

📢 What He Says:

"I'm a really busy person."

🐸 What He Actually Means:

"I'm too busy to prioritize you, but I'll make you feel guilty for asking for any effort."

🔻 UnExpert Tip:
Everyone's busy. If he's really interested, he'll make time — not excuses.

🔊 What He Says:

"I drive a BMW and own 3 businesses."

🐻 What He Actually Means:

"My mom co-signed the car and I sell supplements on Instagram."

🔻 UnExpert Tip:
If he flexes before he speaks, the conversation's over.

🔊 What He Says:

"I don't need a woman — I want one."

🐻 What He Actually Means:

"I'm going to treat you like you're disposable because I think that makes me sound evolved."

🔻 UnExpert Tip:
Wants one... until you want consistency.

🔊 What He Says:

"I'm the type who keeps to himself."

🐻 What He Actually Means:

"I have no communication skills and I think disappearing = masculinity."

🔻 UnExpert Tip:
If he's "quiet," prepare to talk to a wall.

🔊 What He Says:

"I'm a provider."

🦫 What He Actually Means:

"I want control disguised as generosity, and you'll pay for it emotionally."

🔻 UnExpert Tip:
Beware the man who leads with money but hides his morals.

🔊 What He Says:

"I'm still healing from my last relationship."

🦫 What He Actually Means:

"You're now my emotional Band-Aid, therapist, and rebound."

🔻 UnExpert Tip:
Healing is valid. Using you as a stepstool is not.

🔊 What He Says:

"I don't believe in labels."

🦫 What He Actually Means:

"I will act like your boyfriend and deny it every time you bring it up."

🔻 UnExpert Tip:
If he doesn't believe in labels, believe in your exit.

📢 What He Says:

"Let's just see where this goes."

🐸 What He Actually Means:

"I want all the emotional benefits of dating without the responsibility of commitment."

🔻 UnExpert Tip:
He knows where it's going. It's going nowhere.

📢 What He Says:

"I cope with humor."

🐸 What He Actually Means:

"I've never processed anything I've been through and I laugh to avoid actually healing."

🔻 UnExpert Tip:
A good sense of humor is hot. A trauma deflection system? Not so much.

📢 What He Says:

"I want to take care of you."

🐸 What He Actually Means:

"I want control disguised as romance and a quiet thank-you every time I do the bare minimum."

🔻 UnExpert Tip:
If it's love, it won't come with strings — or a tab.

🔊 What He Says:

"I'm just really focused on my career right now."

🐻 What He Actually Means:

"I'm emotionally unavailable but I want to keep you interested just in case."

🔻 UnExpert Tip:
Ambition isn't the problem. Breadcrumbing is.

🔊 What He Says:

"Still figuring out my dating style." *(He's 54.)*

🐻 What He Actually Means:

"I've had multiple marriages, ghosted every situationship since 2009, and still don't know how to use the word 'relationship' in a sentence."

🔻 UnExpert Tip:
At 54, you should be figuring out your *401(k),* not your dating style.

🔊 What He Says:

"Something casual, open to more if there's a connection."

🐻 What He Actually Means:

"I want to hook up guilt-free, but if you catch feelings, I'll pretend I warned you."

🔻 UnExpert Tip:
This is the dating app version of "We'll see 😌" — and you already know what that means.

📢 What He Says:

"Long-term, eventually."

🦹 What He Actually Means:

"I want all the perks of a girlfriend until I feel mildly inconvenienced."

🔻 UnExpert Tip:
"Eventually" is how they keep you invested with no intention of evolving.

📢 What He Says:

"Let's see where it goes."

🦹 What He Actually Means:

"I don't want to lead, but I'll judge you for asking what we are."

🔻 UnExpert Tip:
He knows *exactly* where he wants it to go. And it's usually your bed, not your heart.

📢 What He Says:

"Not sure what I'm looking for, just vibing."

🦹 What He Actually Means:

"I'm here for dopamine hits and external validation until my ex takes me back."

🔻 UnExpert Tip:
If he's not sure, be sure *you* don't get emotionally invested.

📣 What He Says:

"Relationship if the right one comes along."

🐻 What He Actually Means:

"I want a full girlfriend experience without using the word 'girlfriend' in public."

🔻 UnExpert Tip:
Translation: "I'm emotionally unavailable but I'll eat your leftovers and pet your dog."

📣 What He Says:

"Not into labels."

🐻 What He Actually Means:

"I want all the benefits of a committed partner without ever being held accountable like one."

🔻 UnExpert Tip:
If he won't call it anything, it'll never become *anything*.

📣 What He Says:

"Taking things slow."

🐻 What He Actually Means:

"Emotionally unprepared, sexually ready, and commitment allergic."

🔻 UnExpert Tip:
Slow is fine. *Stagnant* is not.

🔊 What He Says:

"I just got out of something..."

🐸 What He Actually Means:

"I'm not ready for anything real, but I'm not about to stop sleeping with you either."

🔻 UnExpert Tip:
Newly out of something = newly unavailable. And often still emotionally *in* it.

🔊 What He Says:

"I'm not in a rush to settle down."

🐸 What He Actually Means:

"I'll take as long as I need to waste your time while casually dating around."

🔻 UnExpert Tip:
"Not in a rush" translates to *I'm dragging this out to see if I can get what I want without any commitment.*

🔊 What He Says:

"I like to keep my options open."

🐸 What He Actually Means:

"I'm here for validation and I want to keep you around just in case nothing else pans out."

🔻 UnExpert Tip:
"Options" are for when you're not emotionally available. If he's keeping his options open, your relationship isn't even on the table.

📢 What He Says:

"I'm not really looking for anything serious right now."

🐸 What He Actually Means:

"I just want to hook up until something better comes along — and you're my temporary distraction."

🔻 UnExpert Tip:
If he's saying this on the first date, don't expect him to change his mind later. This is him being upfront about wasting your time.

📢 What He Says:

"I'm just focusing on myself right now."

🐸 What He Actually Means:

"I'm emotionally unavailable, and you're not a priority, but I still want to keep you around for ego boosts."

🔻 UnExpert Tip:
Focusing on yourself is fine, but focusing on yourself while keeping others as emotional backup is manipulation.

How to Date These Men and Still Win

AKA: *How to Keep the Power When the Vibes Go Weird*

Here's the truth: Some men aren't inconsistent — they're just **very consistent** at *being inconsistent.* They say, "You intimidate me," then punish you for having standards. They "don't believe in labels" but sleep over three nights a week. They'll post gym selfies but vanish when it's time to show up emotionally.

Don't let it shake you. Let it sharpen you.

1. Turn His Inconsistency into Your Clarity

He used to text all the time, now it's sporadic? He made plans once, now he's "busy"?
Perfect. That's not a red flag. That's **data**.

👁 *You're not losing him — you're learning him. And you're not impressed.*

2. Mirror the Disinterest with Classy Indifference

Don't ask him why he's pulling back. Don't beg for consistency.
Just become... elusive.

"Sorry, been slammed. Hope you're well."
Say less. Smile more. He'll feel the shift and chase the energy that's no longer chasing him.

🪓 *Hotter than revenge is radiant indifference.*

3. Challenge His Lines Without Explaining Yourself

He says: "I'm still healing from my ex."
You say: "I hope she gets a refund on the emotional labor."
Then go quiet. No TED Talk. No apology. Just let him sit in it.

✏ *Sometimes the most powerful move is the silence after a mic drop.*

4. Reward Only Aligned Action — Not Promises

He talks about building an empire? Great. Let's see a Google Calendar invite. He says he's "different"? Let him show up on time, plan something, be consistent. Until then, assume it's **just noise**, and spend your time with someone whose behavior matches his hype.

🏗 *Real men build. Fake ones pitch ideas they never start.*

5. Leave First, Leave Beautifully

If you feel the chaos building — the vibes are weird, the words feel hollow, your gut's speaking up — trust it. Exit like a legend. A simple

"This isn't the energy I'm calling in right now, but I wish you the best" can shake a man harder than three months of arguments.

📱 *The woman who walks away without a scene always leaves the strongest impression.*

Final Word for the Chapter 3 Girlies:

Your power is not in **getting him to act right.**
Your power is in how fast you spot the mismatch — and adjust your energy accordingly.

You are not here to beg for clarity. You *are* the clarity.

Every time he fumbles, you upgrade — not because you're mean, but because **you're magnetic.**

Chapter 4: Spiritual Red Flags

When he's "healed" but still toxic.

Welcome to the land of **crystals, cacao, and chaos**. This is the chapter for the guys who say they've done "the work" but can't even apologize correctly. The ones who meditate every morning but somehow still manage to emotionally wreck everyone they date. You'll find them journaling by moonlight, quoting Rumi, and casually dropping how many ayahuasca retreats they've been on — but heaven forbid you ask how they actually treat women.

Spiritual red flags are tricky because they're often **wrapped in self-awareness and sprinkled with therapy words**, but underneath all that sage smoke is usually someone who's more into the *performance of growth* than the actual practice of it. These are the "I'm just protecting my energy" types who ghost without guilt and say it's because "the vibration was off."

Don't get me wrong — growth, healing, and self-reflection are amazing. But when someone uses spirituality to avoid accountability, excuse their inconsistency, or elevate themselves above your very valid needs? That's not conscious. That's just manipulation in mala beads.

This chapter will help you spot the men who **weaponize wellness**, speak in affirmations but act in avoidance, and use "alignment" as a way to never have to commit to anything real.

Let's light a candle and call them out.

📢 What He Says:

"I meditate every morning and journal my intentions."

🐸 What He Actually Means:

"I will gaslight you calmly, then block you with a full moon quote on my story."

🔻 UnExpert Tip:
If his "inner peace" only applies to himself, it's not spiritual — it's selfish.

📢 What He Says:
"I'm just focusing on myself right now."

🐸 What He Actually Means:

"I'm talking to three other women and can't commit to a vibe, let alone a person."

🔻 UnExpert Tip:
"Focusing on myself" is usually code for *"You're plan B."*

📢 What He Says:

"The universe will bring me the right person."

🐸 What He Actually Means:

"I won't pursue you, I won't text back, and I will absolutely blame Mercury for ghosting you."

🔻 UnExpert Tip:
The universe didn't ghost me, babe. You did.

📢 What He Says:

"The gym is my therapy."

🧸 What He Actually Means:

"I have never once gone to actual therapy but I do have strong opinions about protein."

▼ UnExpert Tip:

📢 What He Says:

"I'm really into deep conversations."

🧸 What He Actually Means:

"I'll trauma dump by date two and call it a connection."

▼ UnExpert Tip:
Deep doesn't mean good. It just means *he's unpacking that baggage in your lap.*

📢 What He Says:

"Everything happens for a reason."

🧸 What He Actually Means:

"I refuse to take responsibility and I'm about to emotionally bail."

▼ UnExpert Tip:
This is the spiritual version of *"I'm sorry you feel that way."*

🔊 What He Says:

"I believe in energy."

🐸 What He Actually Means:

"I will sleep with you, burn sage, and vanish without explanation."

🔻 UnExpert Tip:
If the only thing he clears is your contact info, he's not "spiritual," he's sketchy.

🔊 What He Says:

"I'm not perfect, but I'm real."

🐸 What He Actually Means:

"I'm deeply flawed, emotionally unavailable, and want credit for being honest about it."

🔻 UnExpert Tip:
Being "real" isn't a flex if what's real is toxic.

🔊 What He Says:

"I'm an old soul."

🐸 What He Actually Means:

"I still quote Fight Club and think women peaked in the 1950s."

🔻 UnExpert Tip:
You're not an old soul. You're just emotionally undercooked.

📢 What He Says:

"I just feel things really deeply."

🐸 What He Actually Means:

"I'll cry in your arms at 3 a.m. and ghost you by sunrise."

🔻 UnExpert Tip:
Depth means nothing without consistency. He's not deep — he's

---

📢 What He Says:
"I'm really sensitive to energy."

🐸 What He Actually Means:

"I'll pick up on your vibe... and still ignore your boundaries."

🔻 UnExpert Tip:
If he feels everything but *your comfort level,* it's not intuition — it's avoidance with sage.

📢 What He Says:

"I've been hurt in the past."

🐸 What He Actually Means:

"I'm emotionally unavailable, but I want sympathy and attention without actually addressing my trauma."

🔻 UnExpert Tip:
If someone's trauma defines their personality, it's time to walk. You're not their therapist.

How to Date These Men and Still Win
AKA: How to Out-Vibrate a Faux-Woke F*boy Without Losing Your Light

Spiritual men. Love a deep convo. Hate accountability. They'll say, *"I felt your energy shift"* after they cheat. They'll quote Rumi right before they vanish for 11 days. They'll blame their "root chakra imbalance" when they're just emotionally unavailable.

This chapter is for the girlies who saged their room, pulled a card, saw the signs… and still texted him back. We get it. He smelled like Palo Santo and promises. But now? You get to play smarter. Wiser. Way hotter.

---

1. Match His Energy Talk with Grounded Boundaries

If he says, "I'm just really protective of my peace,"
You say: "Me too — that's why I don't chase unclear men."
Spiritual *without* structure is just chaos in mala beads.
🌙 *The vibe is divine and decisive.*

2. Let His Language Reveal His Level

He talks about "mirrors" and "triggers," but never says "I'm sorry"? He references ego deaths but can't handle criticism? Girl, this man's not deep. He's just memorized TikTok therapy.
🔮 *A man who's really done the work will show you peace, not perform it.*

3. Flip the Woo into Warnings

He tells you, "We were meant to cross paths."
Cool. Doesn't mean you were meant to stay. Not every spiritual connection is a soul bond. Some are just well-branded lessons.
🗿 *Just because you feel it doesn't mean you need to feed it.*

4. Stay Rooted, Not Romanticized

If he avoids structure ("Let's just flow, see what happens"),
Set one clear standard and observe his reaction:

"I'm all for flow — but I don't swim in circles."
Spiritual freedom doesn't mean you live in limbo.
📣 *Trust your intuition — not his imagination.*

5. Be the Karmic Upgrade, Not the Lesson

You don't need to fix him, heal him, or help him understand what he did wrong. Your exit will say more than your feedback ever could. If he really is spiritual, he'll reflect on it later — probably in an ayahuasca ceremony.
🌀 *Leave him floating. Ascend without the apology.*

Final Word for the Chapter 4 Girlies:

You are not his mother, his mirror, or his muse.
You're not here to decode the divine on his behalf.
You're a whole portal of power — a walking awakening.
Let him chase his vibration.
You? You chase your **peace, pleasure, and purpose.**

—

Chapter 5: Good-on-Paper Red Flags

When everything checks out — but your gut says "girl, run."

He's successful. He's articulate. He has a job, hobbies, a solid skincare routine, and maybe even a therapist. On paper? He's the dream. But when you're with him, something's *off*. You're second-guessing yourself more than you ever have. You feel low-key judged. He's always "right." And somehow, you're constantly trying to **earn** what already should've felt mutual.

These are the red flags that hide behind a resume — the ones that don't look like red flags until it's way too late. These guys say all the right things, know the buzzwords, and seem emotionally intelligent... until it's time to actually be emotionally available. This chapter is dedicated to the ones who treat dating like an interview, connection like a checklist, and you like a **lifestyle accessory**.

Just because someone looks "ready" for a relationship doesn't mean they're capable of being in one. And just because he says he wants something serious doesn't mean *you're safe* from being strung along.

This chapter will help you spot the difference between a man who's healthy and ready — and one who just **plays the part**.

Let's unpack the résumé red flags.

What He Says:

"I want someone real."

What He Actually Means:

"I'm going to be deeply offended when you have emotions or needs."

UnExpert Tip:
He wants "real" until it requires effort.

What He Says:

"So, what are you looking for?"

What He Actually Means:

"I'm assessing your emotional availability to see how easy it'll be to keep you on the hook with zero effort."

UnExpert Tip:
If he's not leading with what he's looking for, it's because he's just trying to figure out how much of your time he can waste.

What He Says:

"I'm super close with my mom."

What He Actually Means:

"You're about to be in a three-way emotional enmeshment with me and Linda from Long Island."

UnExpert Tip:
There's "respecting your mom," and then there's "needing her permission to buy almond milk."

🔊 What He Says:

"I'm really chill, I go with the flow."

🐸 What He Actually Means:

"I have no plan, no ambition, and I'll let you carry the entire relationship until you burn out."

🔻 UnExpert Tip:

If he's too chill to commit, he's too chill to be your partner.

🔊 What He Says:

"I love strong, independent women."

🐸 What He Actually Means:

"Until you disagree with me or make more money — then I'll get passive-aggressive."

🔻 UnExpert Tip:

🔊 What He Says:

"I'm over my ex; we're still friends though."

🐸 What He Actually Means:

"I still text her when I'm drunk and she still knows my Spotify password."

🔻 UnExpert Tip:
If he's "over it," he shouldn't be revisiting it weekly.

📢 What He Says:

"I'm looking for my best friend."

🐻 What He Actually Means:

"I want someone who'll laugh at my jokes, be available 24/7, and never expect me to initiate intimacy."

🔻 UnExpert Tip:
Best friend is cute — unless he means unpaid emotional support staff.

📢 What He Says:
"Friendship first."

🐻 What He Actually Means:

"I want you to invest emotionally, physically, and spiritually without asking for commitment."

🔻 UnExpert Tip:
It's a *relationship,* not a waiting room.

📢 What He Says:

"Looking for something serious."
(Sends "U up?" at 11:17 AM on a Tuesday.)

🐻 What He Actually Means:

"I know women want something serious, so I'm saying that to get laid faster."

🔻 UnExpert Tip:
If his actions scream hookup and his profile screams husband — believe the actions.

What He Says:

"Wants marriage and kids."
(Also: refuses to date anyone with kids

What He Actually Means:

"I want the fantasy of family life — not the actual effort."

▼ UnExpert Tip:
If he wants "kids someday," but can't handle brunch plans, he's not ready for parenthood — or partnership.

What He Says:

"Emotionally mature and ready to settle down." *(Blocked his last ex for asking what they were.)*

What He Actually Means:

"I know how to spell 'mature,' but not how to practice it."

▼ UnExpert Tip:
Emotional maturity isn't a vibe. It's how he handles your *boundaries.*

What He Says:

"Looking for my person." *(Ghosts you after three weeks of deep convos, a playlist, and meeting your dog.)*

What He Actually Means:

"I love love... until it requires follow-through."

▼ UnExpert Tip:
If "my person" changes monthly, he's not looking — he's collecting.

📢 What He Says:

"I want a real connection." *(Sends "Let's vibe" followed by a mirror selfie with his shirt off.)*

🐀 What He Actually Means:

"I want to feel connected — without being held accountable for your feelings."

🔻 UnExpert Tip:

📢 What He Says:

"I'm not looking to waste time." *(Also refuses to define what he's looking for until month 3.)*

🐀 What He Actually Means:

"I expect you to give me your best while I give the bare minimum — on repeat."

🔻 UnExpert Tip:
If he values time, he won't waste yours. Simple.

📢 What He Is:

Says all his exes were "great people."

🐀 What He Actually Is:

"Has a curated, PR-friendly version of his past and takes zero accountability."

🔻 UnExpert Tip:
If every breakup is someone else's fault — guess who's next?

📢 What He Is:

Polite, punctual, pays for everything.

🪆 What He Actually Is:

"Trains you to confuse basic respect with genuine emotional investment."

🔻 UnExpert Tip:
Bare minimum wrapped in gold still equals *minimum.*
If someone's trauma defines their personality, it's time to walk. You're not their therapist.

📢 What He Is:

Successful, charming, Ivy League educated.

🪆 What He Actually Is:

"Knows how to impress everyone but you emotionally. Weaponizes accomplishments instead of vulnerability."

🔻 UnExpert Tip:
You're not dating his résumé. You're dating his *emotional availability.*
Good grades don't mean good boyfriend.

📢 What He Is:

Takes you to fancy dinners. Plans trips. Spoils you.

🪆 What He Actually Is:

"Uses luxury to cover up his inability to be emotionally generous."

🔻 UnExpert Tip:
Love isn't booked through OpenTable. It's built in the quiet, boring,

🔊 What He Is:

Works out, drinks green juice, meditates.

🐸 What He Actually Is:

"Has mastered health trends but avoids every uncomfortable conversation like it's gluten."

🔻 UnExpert Tip:
Wellness isn't emotional intelligence. He can have abs and still be emotionally constipated.

🔊 What He Says:

"I'm ready to build with someone."
(Also: hasn't replied to a text since Wednesday and doesn't own a bedframe.)

🐸 What He Actually Means:

"I want a girlfriend, therapist, cheerleader, and mom rolled into one. Oh, and bring snacks."

🔻 UnExpert Tip:
If he can't build basic communication, he's not building anything with you.

🔊 What He Is:
Texts good morning, compliments you, never forgets a birthday.

🐸 What He Actually Is:
"Trained in performative romance, but disappears the second emotional intimacy is required."

🔻 UnExpert Tip:
Consistency is only cute if it includes emotional depth — not just *calendar reminders.*

📢 What He Says:

"I don't usually date online."

🐻 What He Actually Means:

"I'm on this app because I'm out of options and need to test the waters. You're my 'what if' date until the real one comes along."

🔻 UnExpert Tip:
He might be emotionally unavailable, or he's just here to pass time. Either way, it's not a good look. Or he is lying and is always dating online and doesn't want you to know his round robin format. I swoon when I hear a guy doesn't date online...and I think they are catching onto that.

📢 What He Is:

Good job. No ex drama. Family man. Doesn't drink.

🐻 What He Actually Is:

"Perfect on paper but incapable of emotional reciprocity. Loves control, not connection."

🔻 UnExpert Tip:
He checks every box but yours. That's not partnership — that's optics.

How to Date These Men and Still Win

AKA: When the Resume Slaps but the Energy Snoozes — Proceed with Hope + Game

He has a great job, no criminal record, solid communication, and maybe even a skincare routine.

But he's awkward. He overshares. He sends "good morning" texts and nothing else.

He loves you in theory but doesn't quite know how to show up in practice.

This chapter is for the girlies who are **tempted to delete Hinge... but not quite yet.**

---

1. Coach Without Coddling

He wants to be better — you can tell. So, give him *the standard,* not *a script.*

Instead of: "It's fine, don't worry about it."

Try: "I appreciate the effort. Next time, just plan it with confidence — I'll show up."

👑 *You're not his mother. You're his mirror with boundaries.*

2. If the Vibe's Off, Say So — Early

He may be nervous, insecure, or unaware. Help him out — kindly but directly.

"You're cute, but don't talk about your ex for 20 minutes again. I'm not her."

This builds trust *and* attraction.

🎯 *Real men rise to direct feedback — not hints.*

3. Don't Confuse Kindness with Chemistry

He's nice. He's sweet. He means well. But if you're bored, unfulfilled, or overcompensating? That's not partnership — it's performance.

Ask: "Do I like *him,* or do I like being liked by him?"

⬚ *Polite isn't enough. Aim for aligned.*

4. If He's Willing, You Can Work with That

The magic phrase: "I like where this is going — but I need a little more clarity/confidence/follow-through."

Say it once, watch his next move. If he levels up? Proceed. If he spirals, sulks, or disappears? You just got your answer — and you didn't waste another week.

🪨 *Teach with presence. Reward with access.*

5. Be the Upgrade, Not the Overhaul

You are not here to overhaul this man into your dream boyfriend.

You're here to **hold the frequency** of the woman who knows her worth.

If he can rise to meet it? Amazing.

If not? You keep walking in heels he'll never be tall enough to fill.

💼 *A resume doesn't equal readiness. Make him prove both.*

Final Word for the Chapter 5 Girlies:

There's hope here — but it's not your job to do the heavy lifting.

You can guide without lowering your standards.

You can stay soft without becoming small.

You're the prize. You're the portal.

If he's smart enough to sense that?

He'll evolve right in front of your eyes.

—

Chapter 6: Comeback Bros

You thought it was over. So did your nervous system. But here he is...
again.

These are the men who ghost, fade, breadcrumb, or flat-out disappear
— only to resurface weeks, months, or even *years* later like nothing
happened. Sometimes it's a casual "hey stranger 👀." Sometimes it's a
dramatic "I've been thinking about you." And occasionally, it's wrapped
in a guilt trip or a faux confession that sounds deep but says *absolutely*
nothing.

Comeback Bros love to reappear just when you've started healing,
thriving, or finally getting over them. It's not a coincidence — it's a
pattern. They thrive on emotional disruption. They want to check if the
door's still open, even though they had no intention of staying in the
first place.

This chapter is your armor against the unexpected re-text, the 2 a.m.
"just thinking about you," and the man who had *zero emotional*
availability last fall but suddenly wants to "catch up" now that the
leaves are turning.

Just because someone circles back doesn't mean they've changed —
most of the time, it just means their ego needs attention... and they
know you used to give it to them.
Let's put up the do-not-disturb sign and keep the door closed this time.

📢 What He Says:

[Disappears for 5 months then texts "Hey you"]

🐸 What He Actually Means:

"The girl I prioritized didn't work out and I'm back to see if your standards dropped."

🔻 UnExpert Tip:
This is not fate. This is ✨recycled attention✨ — block accordingly.

📢 What He Sends:
"I was scared back then."

🐸 What He Actually Means:

"I chose fear over effort, and now I want comfort over closure."

🔻 UnExpert Tip:
Fear is human. But if he hasn't done the work since? That's not fear — that's *still* avoidance.

📢 What He Sends:

👀

🐸 What He Actually Means:

"I have nothing to say but still want attention. Also, I'm probably watching your story from the toilet."

🔻 UnExpert Tip:
The eyes emoji isn't flirting — it's digital loitering.

🔊 What He Sends:
"wyd"

🐻 What He Actually Means:

"I'm bored, horny, or both — but I'll pretend I'm just checking in."

🔻 UnExpert Tip:
If he texts "wyd" more than once a week, he's not a boyfriend — he's background noise.

🔊 What He Sends:

👀 👀 👀 *(with no context)*

🐻 What He Actually Means:

"I saw you posted something cute and I'm hoping you'll chase the breadcrumb."

🔻 UnExpert Tip:
This isn't flirting. It's emotional bait with zero calories.

🔊 What He Sends:

"u up?"

🐻 What He Actually Means:

"I just got bored, horny, and rejected by someone else — so I'm hoping you're still desperate."

🔻 UnExpert Tip:
This isn't a question. It's a test to see if your self-worth is asleep.

📢 What He Sends:

"Hi"
(after disappearing for 3 weeks with zero explanation)

🐻 What He Actually Means:

"I'm circling back to see if the door is still open. No growth, just vibes."

🔻 UnExpert Tip:
You weren't ghosted. You were *archived*. And he just clicked "restore."

📢 What He Says:

"You're such a good person. You deserve someone amazing."
(after emotionally or physically using you)

🐻 What He Actually Means:

"I'm dumping guilt on you so I feel like less of a douchebag."

🔻 UnExpert Tip:
If he *really* thought you were amazing, he wouldn't have treated you like a napkin.

📢 What He Sends:

"Can I come over?"

🐻 What He Actually Means:

"I've made zero effort to know you but I'm banking on your loneliness."

🔻 UnExpert Tip:
If you didn't earn a date, you don't deserve the address.

What He Sends:

"Let me give you a massage."

What He Actually Means:

"I'm disguising sex as self-care."

UnExpert Tip:
If he's not licensed — it's not a massage, it's a strategy.

What He Sends:

"Netflix and chill?"

What He Actually Means:

"We will not finish the movie and I won't text you after."

UnExpert Tip:
If the invite doesn't come with snacks and eye contact, it's not a plan — it's a ploy.

What He Says:

"I didn't mean to hurt you."

What He Actually Means:

"I 100% knew this would hurt you, but I hoped you wouldn't say anything."

UnExpert Tip:
Intent doesn't cancel impact. Especially when the intent was *getting away with it.*

📢 What He Sends:

"Hey stranger 🙄"

🐸 What He Actually Means:

"I ghosted you, circled back, and am now testing your memory and your dignity."

🔻 UnExpert Tip:

📢 What He Sends:
"I miss us."

🐸 What He Actually Means:

"I miss the comfort you gave me without the accountability I avoided."

🔻 UnExpert Tip:
If he missed *you,* he would've showed up when it mattered — not when it was convenient.

📢 What He Sends:

"Was just thinking about you..."

🐸 What He Actually Means:

"I opened my camera roll, saw your face, and remembered I had it good before I blew it."

🔻 UnExpert Tip:
If he's "thinking about you" but not *showing up for you,* let him think in silence.

📢 What He Sends:

"What happened to us?"

🐸 What He Actually Means:

"I'm pretending I don't know exactly how I sabotaged it, so you'll do the emotional labor again."

🔻 UnExpert Tip:
He doesn't want answers — he wants *access.*

📢 What He Sends:

"You crossed my mind today."

🐸 What He Actually Means:

"I was alone with my thoughts and a little too sober — now I need some attention."

🔻 UnExpert Tip:
Crossed his mind? Don't let him *cross your boundaries.*

📢 What He Sends:

"How've you been?"

🐸 What He Actually Means:

"I'm hoping you forgot why you blocked me emotionally, if not physically."

🔻 UnExpert Tip:
If he didn't care then, he doesn't care now — he's just inventory-checking.

📢 What He Sends:

"We had something real."

🐻 What He Actually Means:

"I know I ruined it, but if I call it 'real,' maybe you'll let me back in without consequences."

🔻 UnExpert Tip:
It wasn't "real" if it was one-sided. Romanticizing regret ≠ growth.

📢 What He Sends:

"Are you seeing anyone?"

🐻 What He Actually Means:

"I'm not ready to be serious, but I am ready to interrupt your healing."

🔻 UnExpert Tip:
He doesn't want to date you. He wants to delay your upgrade.

How to Date These Men and Still Win
AKA: *When "Hey Stranger" Might Actually Mean Something — Or Might Mean Run*

Guess who's back? Back again. Shady's back. Tell a friend. The one who ghosted, fizzled, chose chaos... then *remembers you exist* on a random Tuesday. Sometimes it's a genuine check-in.
Sometimes it's emotional dumpster diving. Either way, this chapter is your compass: how to respond, reclaim, or block with grace and greatness.

1. Not All Comebacks Are Created Equal

There's a difference between:

- "Hey. I messed up. I've done some work. Can we talk?"
  ⚪ Worth considering.
  and

- "wyd" at 11:46 p.m.
  ⚫ Worth blocking with joy.

Know the tone. Feel the intention. Energy doesn't lie.

👁 *The more evolved you are, the louder his un-evolved texts will sound.*

2. Look at the Pattern, Not the Potential

Ask yourself:

"Is this the third time he's circled back... or the first?"
"Did anything actually change — or is it just a new month and he's horny again?"
One comeback? Maybe. Three comebacks? You're his comfort zone, not his commitment.

☑ *Growth isn't in the words — it's in the follow-through.*

3. Feelers Are Real — But So Are Boundaries

Some comebacks *are* real feelers. He's nervous. He regrets it. He misses the you that held him to a higher standard. If your gut says there's something left worth exploring, proceed.
But set the tone fast: "I don't entertain confusion twice. What are you actually here for?"

🎯 *A man with real intent will clarify, not dance around it.*

4. If the Opener Is WYD, GTFO

Let's make this universal law: "wyd" = automatic exile.
That's not a check-in. That's an ego scratch. He's not trying to know you again — he's trying to **feel like he still could.**

📝 *You are not his memory. You are his missed opportunity.*

5. Real Men Apologize. Boys Reappear.

The *only* valid comeback is the one with **ownership.**
Not "I miss you,"
Not "I think about you,"
Not "Remember that night…"

But: "I know I hurt you. I regret it. Here's what I've done since — and what I'd love to rebuild."
If he can't say that? He's not back. He's just bored.

⬡ *No redemption without recognition.*

Proceed With Caution Tips:

If you're tempted to reply, run through this checklist:

- Did he disappear before without explanation?

- Has he done any self-work you can *see* (not just say)?

- Has he been consistent since reappearing?

- Do you *trust* yourself not to spiral again?

If yes — maybe he deserves five minutes.
If no — girl, you already know the answer. Screenshot it, laugh about it, block it.

Final Word for the Chapter 6 Girlies:

Sometimes the comeback is real. Sometimes it's just karma sending a little test to see if you've leveled up.

You are not a door to walk through. You're the castle, the key, and the *entire f*cking kingdom.

If he wants in this time — he better knock like a man. Otherwise? He can text "wyd" to the void.

—

Chapter 7: Lovebombers

He says all the right things — and none of it is real.

This is the guy who shows up fast, intense, and "different." He says you're special. That he's never felt this way before. That there's *something about you*. He's planning your future by the second date and calling you "babe" before you've even figured out his last name. It feels like a fairy tale — until it doesn't.

Lovebombers come in hot with compliments, attention, and emotional intimacy — all before any *actual* connection has been built. It's not love. It's **emotional manipulation disguised as romance**. And the goal? To get you attached **fast**, before you have time to see the cracks.

They don't want love. They want **control**. And once they feel like they have you, the energy shifts. Suddenly, they're distant. Confused. Pulling back. You're left wondering what happened — and chasing the version of them they *pretended* to be.

This chapter is here to help you tell the difference between genuine connection and **manufactured intensity**. Because anyone who loves you for who they *think* you are without even knowing you? Isn't looking for love — they're looking for power.
Let's expose the romance ruse.

📣 What He Says:

"You're unlike anyone I've ever met."

🐱 What He Actually Means:

"I say this to anyone who makes eye contact and doesn't run."

🔻 UnExpert Tip:
If you're "different," make sure he's not *exactly the same* as the last five guys.

📣 What He Says:
"Let's take things slow — I want to do this right."

🐱 What He Actually Means:
"I want to sound intentional while secretly avoiding commitment at every turn."

🔻 UnExpert Tip:
"Slow" is fine — if the pace is *honest,* not manipulative.

📣 What He Says:

"I wrote a song about you."

🐱 What He Actually Means:

"I'm going to love-bomb you with lyrics and avoid all real communication."

🔻 UnExpert Tip:
If you get a song before he's learned your last name, run.

🔊 What He Says:
"I've never felt this way before."

🧸 What He Actually Means:

"I'm about to put you on a pedestal and then absolutely shatter it when I lose interest."

🔻 UnExpert Tip:
It's not a feeling — it's a pattern.

🔊 What He Says:

"I'm all in." *(on day 2)*

🧸 What He Actually Means:

"I'm lovebombing the hell out of you because chaos is how I connect."

🔻 UnExpert Tip:
Intensity ≠ intimacy. The faster it starts, the harder it crashes.

🔊 What He Says:

"You're everything I've been looking for."

🧸 What He Actually Means:

"I say this to every woman I date so she lets her guard down."

🔻 UnExpert Tip:
If you're "everything" before he knows anything about you — it's manipulation, not magic.

📢 What He Says:

"I just want to make you happy."

🐸 What He Actually Means:

"I'm a people pleaser with no identity, and I'm going to resent you when I self-abandon."

🔻 UnExpert Tip:
You don't need a martyr. You need a man with a spine and boundaries.

How to Date These Men and Still Win

AKA: *How to Flip the Script on Fast Feelings & Keep Your Power*

He tells you you're "the one" before your appetizer hits the table. He says he's *"never felt this way before."*

He wants to see you every night, meet your mom, move in, **merge souls** — until the moment you say it back. Then? *Poof.* Emotional evacuation. No forwarding address.

Here's how to spot the performance — and protect your power while still enjoying the spotlight.

---

1. Accept the Compliments — But Don't Eat the Bait

Let him gush. Let him adore you. Let him say wild things. But treat it like a preview, not a promise. Smile, sip your drink, and say: "You don't

even know me yet. Wait 'til you see the chaos I bring."
Let him earn the depth — not imagine it.

🕯️ *You're not here for the fireworks. You're here for the fire that stays lit.*

2. Slow It Down — On Purpose

If he's speeding toward forever, slam the brakes gently.
"I move slow when it's real," you say.
This will either expose his need for control... or deepen his respect.

🔋 *Your pace is the standard. If he won't match it, he's not ready for you.*

3. Don't Confuse Intensity with Intention

He might be intense, present, generous — but that doesn't mean he's *stable.* Lovebombing is often about **how he feels about himself** when he's with you, not how he feels about *you.*

💣 *If he's in love by date two, he's projecting — not connecting.*

4. Stay Grounded in Reality, Not Fantasy

While he's talking about babies, weddings, and soul contracts, you stay in the present.
Ask yourself:

"Has he shown emotional consistency?"
"How does he act when I disagree with him?"
"Is he still kind when I have boundaries?"

👁️ *The answers to those questions are sexier than any poem.*

5. If He Pulls Away After You Reciprocate — Laugh.

Seriously. Laugh. Smile. Say: "There it is. Knew it was coming."
Because when you stop chasing and start observing, it's hilarious how

predictable these men are.

🎯 *Let him fade. Then journal about it, post a meme, and glow up.*

Final Word for the Chapter 7 Girlies:

You are not here to be swept away. You are the storm. You don't chase the high — you create the standard. Let the lovebomber perform. You'll be in the front row with popcorn, boundaries, and an exit plan.

Chapter 8: Gaslighters & Word Twisters

If you've ever left a conversation more confused than when you started it — welcome. You've met one.

These are the men who make you question your memory, your emotions, your reactions — *your entire reality*. They never directly insult you, but somehow you always feel like you're overreacting, being too sensitive, or "making things a bigger deal than it is." Sound familiar?

Gaslighting isn't always loud. In fact, it's often subtle, smooth, and performed with a calm tone that makes you look like the unstable one. These men are **experts at flipping the script**. They rewrite arguments. They deflect blame. They say things like *"I never said that"* or *"You're twisting my words."* They'll even "apologize" with lines like *"I'm sorry you feel that way"* — which is basically just emotional warfare in a Hallmark card.

This chapter is your clarity filter. It'll help you recognize the phrases, patterns, and emotional gymnastics used to **manipulate you into silence**, **guilt you into staying**, or **confuse you into thinking it's all your fault**. Spoiler: It's not.

Let's untangle the lies and take your power back — word by word.

🔊 What He Says:

"I'm emotionally unavailable but I'll treat you right."

🦝 What He Actually Means:

"I know I'm the problem. I just don't care enough to fix it."

🔻 UnExpert Tip:
If someone tells you they're unavailable — believe them. You're not a rehab center.

🔊 What He Says:

"You remind me of my ex."

🦝 What He Actually Means:

"I'm emotionally stunted and still not over my ex, so don't expect me to show up for you."

🔻 UnExpert Tip:
Comparison on a first date? Instant red flag. He's not emotionally ready for anyone new.

🔊 What He Says:

"I don't do drama, I do peace."

🦝 What He Actually Means:

"I emotionally check out when you express a valid human feeling."

🔻 UnExpert Tip:
Avoids drama = avoids accountability.

📢 What He Says:
"I don't want to ruin what we have."

🐸 What He Actually Means:

"I like the attention but I'm not willing to give you what you need."

🔻 UnExpert Tip:
If he's protecting the "vibe," he's avoiding the relationship.

📢 What He Says:

"You're overreacting."

🐸 What He Actually Means:

"I'm dismissing your feelings so I don't have to take accountability."

🔻 UnExpert Tip:
Gaslighting starts small. This is one of its favorite opening lines.

📢 What He Says:

"That's not what I said."

🐸 What He Actually Means:

"That is what I said, but now that you're calling me out, I'm rewriting history."

🔻 UnExpert Tip:
He doesn't need a hearing aid. He needs a reality check.

🔊 What He Says:

"You're too emotional."

🗿 What He Actually Means:

"You're reacting like a normal human and it's making me uncomfortable."

🔻 UnExpert Tip:
This is how gaslighters steal your clarity. Don't hand it over.

🔊 What He Says:

"Well, actually..."

🗿 What He Actually Means:

"I'm about to explain something you already know in a tone that'll make you question your intelligence."

🔻 UnExpert Tip:
Mansplaining: because heaven forbid a woman understands anything without his help.

🔊 What He Says:

"Let me explain it better..."

🗿 What He Actually Means:

"I don't think you understood me — not because you didn't, but because you're a woman."

🔻 UnExpert Tip:

📢 What He Says:

"Sorry *you* felt that way."

🏚 What He Actually Means:

"I take no responsibility, but I hope this shuts you up."

🔻 UnExpert Tip:
This isn't an apology — it's an elegant way to call you *too sensitive*.

📢 What He Says:

"That wasn't my intention."

🏚 What He Actually Means:

"I definitely did it, but I'm hoping you'll forgive me based on vibes."

🔻 UnExpert Tip:
Intent ≠ impact. And repeating this line doesn't make him deep — just dodgy.

📢 What He Says:

"I didn't think it would be a big deal."

🏚 What He Actually Means:

"I knew it might hurt you, but not enough to stop myself."

🔻 UnExpert Tip:
If he didn't think, why is *your* heart the one paying the price?

📢 What He Says:

"Let's just move on."

🐻 What He Actually Means:

"I don't want to fix this; I just want you to forget it without resolution."

🔻 UnExpert Tip:
You can't "move on" without repair. This isn't growth — it's emotional skipping stones.

📢 What He Says:

"It's not like I cheated."

🐻 What He Actually Means:

"I crossed every boundary but cheating and want a cookie for restraint."

🔻 UnExpert Tip:
If he's defending his actions by listing what *worse things* he didn't do... RUN.

📢 What He Says:

"I was just in a bad place."

🐻 What He Actually Means:

"My poor choices are now your emotional burden to carry."

🔻 UnExpert Tip:
Healing isn't linear — but hurting others *intentionally* isn't healing at all.

📣 What He Says:

"I'm sorry if I hurt you."

🐻 What He Actually Means:

I don't believe I hurt you, but I'll throw out this vague apology to avoid consequences."

🔻 UnExpert Tip:
If there's an *"if"* in the apology — there's no real accountability.

📣 What He Says:

"You're just being dramatic."

🐻 What He Actually Means:

"I don't take your feelings seriously and I'll invalidate them until you start to believe me."

🔻 UnExpert Tip:
You're not dramatic — he's just allergic to emotional depth.

📣 What He Says:

"I was in a really dark place."

🐻 What He Actually Means:

"Let me emotionally explain away all my red flags instead of being accountable for them."

🔻 UnExpert Tip:
Mental health is real. So is manipulation dressed in vulnerability.

🔊 What He Says:

"I've done a lot of self-reflection."

🐱 What He Actually Means:

"I got dumped, read one self-help quote, and now I think I'm emotionally evolved."

🔻 UnExpert Tip:
If reflection doesn't lead to new behavior — it's just a mirror, not growth.

🔊 What He Says:
"I've learned from my mistakes."

🐱 What He Actually Means:

"I've learned what to say when I want back in. That's it."

🔻 UnExpert Tip:
If he's still repeating the cycle, he didn't learn — he just memorized his lines.

🔊 What He Says:

"I'm working on myself."

🐱 What He Actually Means:

"I'm not in therapy, not reading, not healing — but I am avoiding commitment with flair."

🔻 UnExpert Tip:
Real work is quiet. If he's announcing it, he's probably not doing it.

📣 What He Says:

"I just want to be a better man."

🐸 What He Actually Means:

"I want to sound profound while keeping you emotionally on the hook."

🔻 UnExpert Tip:
A better man doesn't say it — he shows it in how he *treats* you.

📣 What He Says:

"You inspire me to be better."

🐸 What He Actually Means:

"I'll use your emotional labor as my personal development plan... and still let you down."

🔻 UnExpert Tip:
Inspiration is sweet. Accountability is sexier.

📣 What He Sends:

"lol ok"

🐸 What He Actually Means:

"I'm bored, I'm pretending I'm laughing, but I really just want you to stop talking."

🔻 UnExpert Tip:
"lol" is his way of staying in your life without actually participating in it.

📢 What He Sends:

"Sorry you feel that way."

🪆 What He Actually Means:

"I'm not sorry for what I did. I'm just blaming you for how I made you feel."

🔻 UnExpert Tip:
This isn't an apology. It's him shifting the blame so he doesn't have to take responsibility.

How to Date These Men and Still Win

AKA: Proceed with Caution — Because You're Not Crazy, Sis

Here's the tricky thing about gaslighting: You don't know it's happening until you're doubting your own damn instincts. He'll say you're "overthinking," that you're "too sensitive," or that he "didn't mean it like that" — right after he *very much* meant it like that.

Some gaslighters are smooth manipulators. Others? Just emotionally stunted. But regardless of intent, the impact is the same: **you start shrinking.**

Not anymore. You're about to **trust your perception like it's gospel.**

---

1. When In Doubt, Zoom Out

If you're starting to question your reactions constantly, ask yourself:
"Would my best friend feel the same way in this situation?"
This removes emotion and brings clarity. Because if *everyone* would be confused by his mixed messages?

👁️🗨️ *It's not you. It's the fog he's creating.*

2. Set a Reality Anchor Before You Engage

Before a heavy convo, write down exactly what happened and how it made you feel. Then see how he reacts when you bring it up. If he twists the facts, blames your tone, or starts spinning the convo back on you? That's a red flag in slow motion.

⚖️ *Clarity doesn't need a defense. Watch for the spin.*

3. Don't Debate Reality — Hold It Steady

Gaslighters *thrive* on emotional confusion. So when he says, *"That's not what I meant,"* or *"You're being dramatic,"* you say: "Intent doesn't erase impact."
Say it once, then stop. Don't explain, don't spiral. Let him sit with it.
▢ *Your version of reality is valid. Protect it like your peace.*

4. Watch for the Apology That Feels Like an Attack

The classic gaslighter move: "I'm sorry **you** feel that way."
That's not an apology. That's emotional misdirection. Only accept apologies that include **ownership**: "I understand how I hurt you. I'll do better."
If he can't give you that? He's not safe for your softness.

📱 *Low-level gaslighting over time will wreck your self-trust. Leave before that.*

5. When It Feels Subtle, Pay Even More Attention

Not all gaslighting looks like a blow-up. Sometimes it's small: forgetting things you clearly said, denying tone, rewriting arguments. These "little things" are designed to make you **doubt your emotional compass**.

🔔 *Caution: This is how your intuition gets muted. Turn the volume back up.*

Proceed with Caution Tips:

If you're not sure he's gaslighting you... here's your checklist:

- Do you feel more confused after talking to him than before?

- Do you keep second-guessing how you "should've said it"?

- Do you walk on eggshells trying to say things "the right way"?

- Do you feel like you have to bring evidence just to be heard?

If any of those hit? You don't need to fight about it. You just need to **start emotionally stepping back**. Observe more. Invest less. Hold your truth tighter.

Final Word for the Chapter 8 Girlies:

You are not "too sensitive."
You're *finally* sensing something for real.
You don't need to win an argument — you need to **win your own peace of mind** back.

Let him gaslight himself. You've got better places to be.

—

Chapter 9: Coded Narcissists

He speaks fluent therapy, but none of it touches his soul.

This is the chapter for the men who've mastered the **language of healing** — but not the practice. The ones who say all the right things: *"I've done the work," "I've really grown," "I'm in tune with my emotions."* They'll quote Brene Brown, talk about "holding space," and casually mention their last therapist... yet still somehow make you feel like the unstable one when things get hard.

Coded narcissists hide behind spiritual lingo, self-awareness, and emotionally intelligent phrasing to appear evolved while still operating from deep dysfunction. They don't yell. They don't insult. They just **drain you slowly**, one mindfulness buzzword at a time.
What makes them dangerous is that they're convincing. They believe their own script.

And because they say things that *sound* good, you start to question your gut instead of their behavior. These aren't the obvious narcissists — these are the ones who manipulate with a calm tone, a soft voice, and an IG feed full of quotes about growth.

This chapter will help you spot the ones who've **rebranded toxicity as self-awareness** — and remind you that real emotional health isn't something you talk about. It's something you live.

Let's decode the self-proclaimed "good guys."

📢 What He Says:

"I spoil my woman." Or in my case "I spoil you."

🐻 What He Actually Means:

"I buy you one dinner and use it as leverage until 2026."

🔻 UnExpert Tip:
If he says "spoil," ask: with what? Attention? Affection? DoorDash?

📢 What He Says:

"I'm a really good listener."

🐻 What He Actually Means:

"I'll nod and make eye contact while you talk, but I'm really just waiting for my turn to talk about me."

🔻 UnExpert Tip:
If the "listener" talks about themselves constantly, they're not actually listening. They're just waiting for their moment to shine.

📢 What He Says:

"You deserve someone better than me."

🐻 What He Actually Means:

"I already know I'm going to hurt you and this is my pre-written excuse."

🔻 UnExpert Tip:
When they *tell* on themselves? Listen.

📢 What He Says:
"I've done a lot of work on myself."

🐻 What He Actually Means:

"I read two books and now think I'm qualified to critique your healing journey."

🔻 UnExpert Tip:
True growth is quiet — not constantly advertised.

📢 What He Says:

"I'm not like other guys — I actually care."

🐻 What He Actually Means:

"I've mastered the art of sounding emotionally intelligent while still avoiding all actual accountability."

🔻 UnExpert Tip:
Words ≠ growth. Watch what he *does*, not what he claims.

📢 What He Says:

"That's not who I am anymore."

🐻 What He Actually Means:

"I'm hoping you'll forget what I did and give me a second chance to do it better... or worse."

🔻 UnExpert Tip:
New vibe, same chaos. Don't be the test run for his "growth era."

📢 What He Is:

Doesn't fight. Ever. Always stays "calm."

🐻 What He Actually Is:

"Avoids conflict at all costs, represses emotion, and quietly resents you until he vanishes without warning."

🔻 UnExpert Tip:
Calm ≠ healthy. Communication without expression is just silence with eye contact.

🪦 Do NOT Date These Men and Still Win
AKA: There Is No Redemption Arc — Only Escape

Some red flags you can laugh at. Some men you can finesse, outsmart, redirect, or even heal with time.

But not this one.

This chapter is not about dating smarter — it's about **survival.** Because once you've met a narcissist, especially the kind who wears charm like cologne and reads leadership books like bibles — you will never forget the cost of ignoring your gut.

🚫 There's No Safe Way to Date a Coded Narcissist

They don't get "better."
They get better at **hiding it.**

They know exactly how to win your trust, mirror your dreams, and make you feel like *you're the lucky one.* They'll say they've never met anyone like you — and they haven't. But that doesn't mean they value you. It means they see potential for control.

They're often leaders. Bosses. Coaches. Salesmen. They read *How to Win Friends and Influence People* and weaponize it. They know how to work a room, disarm suspicion, and keep you addicted to their approval.

They always leave behind a **trail of women who are too ashamed to speak.**

And I know. Because I was one of them.

💜 My Story (A True One — Not Just a Warning)

I hate the term narcissist. I think it is absolutely overused in today's dating. Women mistake carelessness as narcissism. No. Women portray men in "Are We Dating the Same Guy" as narcissists, when the women are in fact the true narcissists. There isn't a fine line, here. This isn't a blanket, these are true manipulators who take your soul, not ones who just didn't feel a connection anymore. These men used you until they couldn't use you anymore. So please, ladies, I beg of you, do not use the word Narcissist without truly knowing the meaning of the word. Narcissists are literally humans without a soul. Think of it that way. They do not care about anybody but themselves.

One narcissist was my boss. He pulled me in with admiration, flattery, and "potential."

He destroyed my job, my finances, my stability — and then cut me loose the second I was no longer beneficial (and found out he was sleeping with one of our vendors). On the upside to losing everything, my dream job, my career. Because why would anyone hire a woman who whored around with her boss? I decided not to let that eat at me. Trust me it ate at me for a month. Applying for every job and getting no interviews.

But I found my redemption. I have always wanted to be a writer, was a writer, and some of you have read my other books. This is my redemption. This is me going full force into my dream and not stopping. Since I was in third grade, and wrote my first script, I wanted to be a screenwriter, and now I am not stopping. I believe in myself more than ever and know this was my destiny. I am finally not afraid if I fail, because at least I know I tried with every once of my being.

If you learn anything from this book, is that you can do anything you put your heart and soul into. If you are searching, watch this video: https://www.youtube.com/watch?v=s8nFACrLxr0&t=554s (I have no affiliation with this film, it was brought to my attention in my darkest hours, the hours I thought about leaving, yes that leaving, and it brought back my flame. It might not do the same for you, but watch it. And if you are ever in that place, please email me at yourdatingunexpert@gmail.com we will find your bliss. Again, I am not a therapist, I'm just your girlfriend. So, if you need actual help, please find one in your area. There are some that also work with low-income families, or schools with students needing to get their clinical hours.)

My next favorite narcissist, was a three-and-a-half-year mistake, where I should have known after month three, he was going to destroy me. He was the ultimate lovebomber. Wanted to marry me after month one...I mean duh, I am flipping amazing. He built me up, planned our future, and got me to trust him with my time, my body, my *money*.

'm still owed $7,000.

I'm not getting it back — but I got my *self* back. And that's worth everything.

The third story I wrote into a script called **Manipulation.** This is a true story, and the darkest levels of what a narcissist is capable of will do. And that is murder.

That's not drama. That's not metaphor. That's **how far this pattern can go** when you ignore the signals and keep believing the potential.

How to Tell It's Calculated

We all have narcissistic traits. But narcissistic **personality disorder** is **deliberate deception wrapped in charisma.** Here's how you know it's not just immaturity:

- He flatters you before he even knows you.

- He escalates commitment fast — lovebomb style — but with *surgical* precision.

- He isolates you emotionally by making you feel like **he's the only one who "gets you."**

- He talks a lot about empathy, growth, and leadership — but **never takes true accountability.**

- When he hurts you, it's always your fault. When he's called out, he turns it into *his* victim story.

He's convincing. He's intelligent. He might even be beloved by others. But he is dangerous. Not because he's angry — but because he is **empty.**

90

🪦 There's No Power Move Here. Just Leave.

This is the only chapter where I won't tell you how to make it work.

Because **it's not supposed to.**

You don't beat a narcissist by being clever.
You don't "mirror his energy" or "set better boundaries."
You **exit. Swiftly. Quietly. Fully.**

And when he circles back — and he always does — *you don't answer.*
You remember that your nervous system is **finally healing.**

You remember that the part of you who once would've replied…
is the version of you **he destroyed.**

Final Word for the Chapter 9 Girlies:

Please, I am begging you. **Never date a narcissist.** It doesn't make you stronger. It makes you lose yourself. And sometimes, it costs you more than you think you can recover from.

There are men who are clumsy, confused, even selfish — but they can grow.
A narcissist doesn't grow. He *studies you. Repeats patterns. Evolves manipulation.*

You don't need to decode him. You need to *run like your life depends on it.*

Because sometimes?

It actually does.

Chapter 10: Red Flags You Ignored on Purpose

You saw it. You knew it. You just... didn't want to deal with it.

This is the chapter we don't write for revenge — we write it for **redemption**. Because if you've ever justified a walking red flag with *"But he's been through a lot,"* or *"The sex is really good,"* or *"He's just not used to someone like me,"* — babe, you're not alone.

Sometimes the flag wasn't even subtle. It was blinding. Waving in slow motion. Set to dramatic music. And yet... you stayed. You waited. You hoped. You chose potential over reality. And honestly? That doesn't make you weak. That makes you **human**.

This chapter is about the red flags you *wanted* to be wrong about. The ones you tried to explain away. The ones you held on to because letting go felt lonelier than the confusion. It's not about shaming yourself — it's about finally calling it what it was, so you never tolerate it again.

This is your permission slip to forgive yourself, laugh a little (or cry a lot), and swear on everything holy: **never again**.

Let's call out the ones you saw coming — and chose to love anyway.

🔊 **What He Says:**

"I'm done with games."
(Immediately tries to test you with dry replies, jealousy comments, or ghosting and returning like a boomerang.)

🐻 **What He Actually Means:**

"I'm the game."

🔻 **UnExpert Tip:**
If you have to decode every text — it's not connection, it's a crossword puzzle with commitment issues.

🔊 **What He Says:**
"I've been told I'm intimidating."
🐻 **What He Actually Means:**
"I conflate arrogance with confidence and nobody has corrected me yet."

🔻 **UnExpert Tip:**
Real confidence is quiet. If he leads with ego, prepare for volume — not value.

🔊 **What He Says:**
"My friends say I'm a lot."

🐻 **What He Actually Means:**
"Chaos is my love language, and I think it makes me interesting."

🔻 **UnExpert Tip:**
Hot mess energy is fun — until your nervous system files a restraining order.

📢 **What He Says:**

"I'm emotionally available *for the right person.*"

🐻 **What He Actually Means:**

"I'm available for vibes, validation, and attention — not accountability."

🔻 **UnExpert Tip:**

If he can't show up now, you're not the exception. You're the emotional test drive.

📢 **What He Says:**

"I'm not really on here much."

🐻 **What He Actually Means:**

"I've been ghosting women across three platforms and don't want to be held accountable here either."

🔻 **UnExpert Tip:**

He's on enough to message *you,* so don't romanticize it. If he's too busy to type, he's too busy to date.

📢 **What He Says:**

"I'm an open book."

🐻 **What He Actually Means:**

Except the chapters with his ex, his avoidant issues, his financial reality, or why he actually left his last relationship.

🔻 **UnExpert Tip:**

Ask the right question and watch him suddenly become a Choose-Your-Own-Adventure full of plot holes.

📢 **What He Says:**

"I'm a really private person."

🐻 **What He Actually Means:**

"You'll never meet my friends, post me, or know what I'm really doing, but I'll still call you clingy."

🔻 **UnExpert Tip:**

Privacy is sacred. Secrecy is strategy. Know the difference.

📢 **What He Says:**

"I'm not really a texter."

🐻 **What He Actually Means:**

"I want attention when I'm bored but won't provide consistency or clarity."

🔻 **UnExpert Tip:**

You're not a carrier pigeon. If he can't form a full sentence, he's not ready for a full woman.

How to Date These Men and Still Win

AKA: I Know He's Chaos, But He's My Little Chaos — For Now

Sometimes a red flag isn't dangerous — it's just... *inconvenient.* He plays too many video games. He listens to podcasts. He refuses to drink oat milk. He's 5'10 but says he's 6'0. His ex still follows him. His Spotify Wrapped was a *little* too EDM.

And you know it.

You *see it.*

But you still answer his texts with a little smile on your face like:

"Shut up, you're annoying."

(Translation: "I'm obsessed with you and I'll pretend I'm not.")

This chapter is for the women who are **self-aware enough to clock the nonsense** and **confident enough to decide what actually matters.**

---

1. Know Your Line Between 'Red' and 'Just Beige'

Not every imperfection is a dealbreaker. Some things are just *quirks.* The key? Knowing **which ones you're tolerating vs. which ones you're excusing.** If it annoys you but doesn't harm you — fine. If it chips away at your self-worth? Run.

🖊 *You're allowed to date a little messy. Just not toxic.*

2. Don't Try to Fix What You're Tolerating

You can't date him for the *vibes* and then try to **turn him into husband material** mid-way through. If he's just for fun — leave it at fun. Don't change his playlist, his wardrobe, or his brain.

🕸 *Not every man is a forever man. Some are just your summer soundtrack.*

3. Let Yourself Have a Flawed Crush — But Keep One Eye Open

Go on the date. Flirt with the walking red flag. Let him charm you. But stay **just aware enough** to leave when it stops being fun.

👁 *The emotionally mature woman knows how to tap out early — with lashes still on and dignity intact.*

4. Tell Your Friends the Truth So You Don't Gaslight Yourself Later

Tell your bestie: "I know he's annoying. I'm ignoring it on purpose. Please don't let me romanticize this in two weeks."
It's called **safety net dating.** We love an accountability circle.

📱 *Group chat transparency saves lives.*

5. Leave While It's Still Cute

The #1 tip for ignoring small red flags? **Know when to leave before they become big ones.**
Sometimes, the hottest exit is the one you make *before the disappointment starts.*

🗡 *Leave him with a compliment and a blocked number. Icon behavior.*

Final Word for the Chapter 10 Girlies:

You're not stupid for texting him.
You're not weak for giving him a shot.
You're human. You're hot. You're curious.

Just don't mistake **chaotic neutral** for a love story.
Have your fun — but **don't build a future out of vibes.**

If you're going to ignore red flags, do it with clear eyes, a sharp lip, and an escape plan.

Part Three: What to Do After You Spot a Red Flag

Because seeing it is step one. Walking away is the power move.

Don't Ignore It

Let's start here — with the hardest part: **acknowledging what you already know**.

You saw the red flag. You felt the shift. Something in your body whispered, *"This isn't right,"* and your brain probably tried to reason it away. That's normal. Especially when the chemistry is good, the potential feels high, or they're offering you just enough to keep you hooked.

But ignoring red flags doesn't make them go away — it just makes them more expensive. In time. In energy. In self-worth. Every time you ignore one, you're not just giving them a pass — you're **teaching yourself to doubt your own instincts**.

So, the rule is simple: **believe it the first time**. Don't wait for more evidence. Don't wait for the apology. Don't wait for your boundaries to be crossed twice. You don't need things to get worse to justify walking away.

A red flag is enough.

Reclaim Your Power

Red flags don't just point to what's wrong with them — they point to what needs protecting in **you**.

The moment you recognize a red flag and act on it, you are no longer in the passenger seat of your dating life. You are making a conscious decision to **choose yourself**, even when it's uncomfortable. That's power.

Reclaiming your power doesn't always look loud. Sometimes it's quietly blocking a number. Sometimes it's not responding to the "hey stranger" text. Sometimes it's writing a note to your future self that says *"We don't go back anymore."*

Power is not proving your worth. Power is **knowing your worth** — and refusing to negotiate it with someone who doesn't see it.

Trust Your Gut

Your intuition is never wrong. Ever.

It's the part of you that senses when something's off, even when your mind is trying to convince you otherwise. The body always knows. The unease, the tension, the subtle drop in your energy — that's your internal compass trying to protect you.

Trusting your gut doesn't mean you'll never make a mistake. It means you'll never **stay** in something that isn't aligned just because someone else wants you to. It means you stop outsourcing your clarity to people who benefit from your confusion.

Here's your permission slip to trust yourself fully:
You don't need more proof.
You don't need to ask three friends.
You don't need to wait until it hurts more.

You already know. And that's enough.

The Red Flag After Party

You spotted the flags. You walked away. Now you celebrate like the emotionally evolved savage you are.

You've made it through the chaos, the lovebombs, the vague texts, the therapy-speak narcissists, and the "sorry if I hurt you" men. This section is for **reclaiming your voice, rewriting your story**, and throwing confetti over every red flag you now dodge in heels.

💬 Red Flag Comeback Lines

Because sometimes the best closure is *no response*.
And other times? You go full cinematic mic drop.

"You lost me at 'let's take it slow.'"
"Tell your situationship I said hi."
"I'm not confused — I'm just not interested."
"Your communication style? Ghost with Wi-Fi."
"My intuition said no before you finished typing."

📷 Screenshots You Should've Blocked *(Sample Edition)*

Feel free to replace these with real crowd-sourced ones later, but for now:

Message: *"You up?"*
Blocked Energy Reply: "No, but my standards are."

Message: *"Why are you being so distant lately?"*
Blocked Energy Reply: "Just trying to match your availability, king."

Message: *"I'm not like other guys."*
Blocked Energy Reply: "You're right — some of them actually try."

🌿 Affirmations for Women Who've Had Enough

"I don't romanticize red flags. I remove them."

"My peace is the prize. Not his potential."

"I no longer date maybes."

"I'm not hard to love — just hard to manipulate."

"I'm not the one. I'm the warning."

🏷️ Dating App Bio Obituaries

Because some bios need to be laid to rest.

Here lies: "6'2 because apparently that matters."
Died trying to weaponize his height against your standards.
May he rest in passive-aggressive bitterness.

Here lies: "Looking for a best friend and a vibe."
Never defined either.
Buried under 147 unopened chats and one ex still on his couch.

Here lies: "I don't do drama, I do peace."
Gaslit 12 women into thinking their feelings were conflict.
Survived by three muted group chats.

Final Word: You're Not Crazy — You're Finally Clear

Let's be real — you didn't read this book just to laugh at the red flags (although... worth it).
You read this book because **you've been gaslit, lovebombed, led on, and left confused**, more times than you'd like to admit.
You've silenced your gut to make space for someone else's chaos.
You've called it "patience" when it was actually self-betrayal.
You've waited for them to choose you while forgetting you already had a choice.

But not anymore.

You don't need another half-grown man explaining how he's "working on himself."
You don't need another late-night voice memo, another almost-relationship, another text that leaves you spiraling.
You don't need another excuse to ignore what your body is already telling you.

You need truth. You need peace.
You need to look at a red flag and say, **"No thanks. I've met your type before."**
And then walk away — **with your standards intact and your self-worth unshaken.**

So, here's your final reminder:
You're not too much.
You're not hard to love.
You're not "just dramatic."

You're just done settling.
And if that scares them? Let them run.

You?
You've got red flag vision now.
And you're not looking back.

🙏 Final Toast — A Dedication

For every woman who got ghosted and *didn't let it haunt her.*
For the one who cried, healed, glowed up, and *never texted back.*
For the ones who ignored their intuition — until they learned to **honor it like gospel**.
For you — the reader, the legend, the woman who's officially done accepting crumbs and calling it chemistry.

This isn't just a book.
This is your receipt.
This is your reminder.
This is your rebirth.

Here's to red flags — and the women who learned to run faster.